Walter Einstein

Seizing Success: Investment Opportunities for Young Adults

First edition

This book was professionally typeset on Reedsy
Find out more at reedsy.com

To my readers,
I dedicate this book to each and every one of you, the ambitious young adults
who are eager to take control of your financial future. You possess a burning
desire to make your hard-earned money work for you, and this dedication is a
testament to your unwavering commitment to personal growth and financial
success.
With gratitude

"An investment in knowledge pays the best interest."

Benjamin Franklin

Contents

    1.

    2.

    3.

    4.

    5.

    6.

    7.

    8.

    9.

    10.

    11.

    12.

    13.

    14.

15.

16.

Preface

Welcome to "Seizing Success: Investment Opportunities for Young Adults." I specifically designed this book to equip you with the knowledge and tools necessary to navigate the world of investing and make informed decisions that can shape your financial future.

Investing is an amazing asset that can assist you with accomplishing your monetary objectives, whether it's structure riches, subsidizing your fantasy business, purchasing a home, or resigning easily. Nonetheless, it's essential to perceive that contributing isn't saved by the well-off or experienced experts alone. There are various venture valuable open doors accessible explicitly customized for youthful grown-ups.

This book fills in as a far-reaching guide, furnishing you with useful experiences, techniques, and assets to profit from this speculation and potentially open doors. It is intended to engage you with the information to settle on certain speculation choices, regardless of your related knowledge or foundation.

The book centres on building areas of strength for an establishment. We'll investigate the significance of defining objectives, making a spending plan, and overseeing obligations to lay out a strong monetary balance. Without a strong groundwork, contributing can be hazardous and less successful. In this way, how about we lay the preparation for your monetary achievement?

It dives into the rudiments of effective money management. It talks about different speculation choices, like stocks, securities, common assets, and retirement accounts. Understanding these essentials will empower you to go with informed choices regarding resource assignment and expansion.

The book additionally investigates venture potential open doors explicitly custom-made for youthful grown-ups. From securities exchange, and effective money management to land, distributed loaning, influence money management, and elective ventures like digital currencies and substantial resources, we'll cover many choices to assist you with tracking down an ideal choice for your monetary objectives and hazard hunger.

addresses the difficulties that accompany money management. Overseeing risk, dealing with feelings, and exploring charge contemplations are urgent parts of turning into an effective financial backer. Furthermore, we'll examine long-haul money management systems and retirement wanting to guarantee that you have a guide for supported monetary development.

The book likewise shares useful hints, contextual investigations, and master bits of knowledge to give you a balanced comprehension of the speculation scene. This book plans to furnish you with the essential instruments and information to settle on all-around informed choices, yet a definitive obligation lies with you.

I need to underline that you are in good company on this excursion. As a youthful grown-up, you enjoy the benefit of time and the potential for compound development. By beginning early, going with savvy venture decisions, and ceaselessly adjusting your procedures, you have the potential chance to make monetary progress and security.

Keep in mind, this book is only the start of your speculation process. It is intended to rouse and teach, however, the genuine worth lies in making a move and applying what you realize. In this way, I urge you to make a plunge, investigate the parts, get clarification on pressing issues, look for additional information, and assume command over your monetary future.

Wishing you the greatest amount of outcome in your speculation tries!

1

Grasping the Force of Investing

First and foremost, investing allows your money to work for you rather than just sitting in a savings account. By putting your money into various investment vehicles such as stocks, mutual funds, real estate, or even starting your own business, you have the potential to generate significant returns over time.

One of the critical standards of money management is taking a drawn-out viewpoint. While there might be transient changes and market slumps, history has shown that the financial exchange, for instance, has reliable areas of strength for conveyed long term. By remaining contributed as long as possible, you can profit from intensifying returns, where your income produces extra income, prompting dramatic development.

Diversification is one more significant perspective to consider investing. It includes spreading your speculations across an assortment of resource classes, ventures, or geographic districts. Diversification lessens risk by trying not to tie up your assets in one place. Assuming that one venture fails to meet expectations, the others can take care of equilibrium it, limiting likely misfortunes.

Timing is a vital component with regard to effective investing. Attempting to time the market impeccably is almost unthinkable. Rather than endeavouring to purchase at the absolute bottom and sell at the most noteworthy, it's expected more judicious to zero in on your drawn-out objectives and contribute reliably, paying little mind to economic situations. Someone regularly known this technique as minimizing risk, and it helps smooth out market unpredictability and decreases the gamble of going with profound speculation choices.

One more urgent part of investing is remaining educated and taught. Staying aware of monetary news, understanding industry drifts, and investigating potential speculation amazing open doors can assist you with pursuing more educated choices. It's in every case great to talk with a monetary consultant or do your own exploration prior to settling on any speculation choices.

The fact that investing implies taking a chance makes, at long last, it memorable's essential. While there's the true capacity for significant returns, there's likewise the chance of losing cash. It's significant to survey your gamble resistance and contribute in a like manner. A differentiated portfolio with a blend of safe and high-risk ventures can assist with moderating likely misfortunes.

Investing is a useful asset that can assist you with developing your abundance over the long haul. By taking a drawn-out viewpoint, broadening your ventures, contributing reliably, remaining informed, and understanding your gamble resistance, you can tackle the force of investing to accomplish your monetary goals.

Why Investing Matters for Young Adults

As a young grown-up, you might end up shuffling numerous monetary obligations, for example, understudy loans, leases, and everyday costs. With this large number of prompt requirements and requests on your pay, investing probably won't be extremely important to you. Understanding the significance of investing from the get-go can altogether affect your future monetary prosperity. Here's the reason investing matters for young adults:

1. Time and Compound Interest: Time is a powerful partner regarding investing. The previous you begin investing, the more drawn out your cash needs to develop, because of the force of compound interest. Compound interest permits your underlying speculation to acquire returns, which then reinvest and procure significantly more returns. Over the long run, this compounding impact can essentially increase your riches. By beginning early, you can make the most of this remarkable development and possibly accomplish your monetary objectives sooner.

2. Retirement Arranging: While retirement could appear to be a far-off idea when you're simply beginning your vocation, making arrangements for it early is critical. As a matter of fact, beginning to put something aside for retirement in your twenties or thirties can have an enormous effect in the personal satisfaction you'll have during your brilliant years. By investing in retirement records, for example, a 401(k) or Individual Retirement Record (IRA), you can exploit tax breaks while developing your reserve funds after some time. The prior you start contributing, the additional time your ventures need to amass and compound.

3. Creating Financial momentum: Investing permits you to create financial well-being past what you could accomplish through ordinary reserve funds techniques alone. While setting aside cash in a normal ledger is fundamental for crises and transient objectives, it's essential to perceive that the profits on investment accounts are ordinarily negligible. By investing, you might possibly acquire better yields and increment your abundance over the long haul. This can give you monetary security, open up open doors for accomplishing your fantasies, and permit you to make a more agreeable future for yourself as well as your friends and family.

4. Expansion Security: Expansion dissolves the buying influence of your cash after some time. By investing in resources that have outperformed expansion, for example, stocks or land, you can safeguard your abundance from the effects of rising costs. By developing your ventures at a rate that outperforms expansion, you're bound to keep up with the buying influence of your cash and save your monetary prosperity over the long haul.

5. Creating Monetary Proficiency: Investing gives a superb chance to develop monetary education and create a more profound

Conquering Normal Investing Confusions for Young Adults

Investing can be scary, particularly for young adults who might not have a lot of involvement or information in monetary issues. Notwithstanding, it's vital for move past normal confusions to exploit the advantages that investing can offer. The following are a couple of misguided judgments to survive:

1. Investing is just for the well-off: One of the most predominant misinterpretations is that investing is just for the people who have a truckload of cash in excess. Notwithstanding, this couldn't possibly be more off-base. You needn't bother with it to be affluent to begin investing. Numerous speculation choices are open to individuals with various pay levels. Whether you're beginning with a limited quantity or step by step expanding your speculations over the long haul, the significant thing is to begin as soon as conceivable to exploit compounding interest and create financial momentum over the long haul.

2. Investing is excessively unsafe: Another normal confusion is that investing is excessively dangerous, and your well-deserved cash will vanish for the time being. While it is actually the case that investing implies some level of hazard, it's vital to comprehend that gambling and awards remain forever inseparable. By broadening your ventures and doing exhaustive exploration, you can oversee and moderate dangers. It's additionally critical to contribute for the long haul as opposed to attempting to time the market. After some time, the financial exchange has generally displayed vertical development, and remaining contributed through market vacillations has demonstrated to be a successful system.

3. I'm excessively young to begin investing: Numerous young adults accept they have a lot of time to contribute and that it's something they can stress over later. Nonetheless, as referenced prior, time is a significant component with regard to investing. Beginning early permits you to bridle the force of compounding interest and exploit market development over the long haul. The more extended your speculations need to develop, the more prominent the likely returns. Thus, don't hang tight for the "great" time to begin investing — begin now and let time help you out.

By understanding the force of investing and exposing normal misguided judgments, young adults can acquire trust in their capacity to leave on a successful venture and secure their monetary future.

2

Putting Forth Monetary Goals

Monetary success starts with putting forth clear and attainable goals. In this part, we will investigate the significance of characterizing both present-moment and long-term monetary goals and how they add to building areas of strength for an establishment.

Characterizing Present Moment and Long-Term Goals

Understanding the distinction between the present moment and long-term goals is critical while laying out a monetary guide. Transient goals commonly range one year or less and frequently include quick monetary requirements or want. Instances of momentary goals incorporate making a secret stash, taking care of charge card obligations, or putting something aside for a getaway.

Then again, long-term goals are those that reach out past a year and typically rotate around significant life achievements or accomplishments. These goals frequently require more significant monetary preparation and responsibility. In instances of long-term goals, remember to putting something aside for an initial investment in a house, finance advanced education, or build retirement savings.

Making a Sensible Monetary Arrangement

Whenever you have recognized your present moment and long-term goals, now is the right time to make a reasonable monetary arrangement to accomplish them. Here is a move to guide you all the while:

Stage 1: Survey what is happening: Check out your pay, costs, resources, and liabilities. Grasp your income and distinguish regions where you can get acclimations to let loose more cash flow for your goals.

Stage 2: Focus on your goals: Figure out which goals are vital to you and focus on them appropriately. Think about the time skyline, monetary responsibility, and individual meaning of every objective.

Stage 3: Set explicit and quantifiable targets; Make your goals explicit and quantifiable. For instance, rather than saying, "I need to set aside cash," set an objective like, "I need to save $5,000 for an initial instalment on a house in the following two years."

Stage 4: Separate your goals into reasonable advances: Gap your goals into more modest achievements or activities that you can achieve en route. This helps track progress and keep up with inspiration.

Stage 5: Decide the assets required: evaluate the monetary assets expected to accomplish every objective. Consider factors, for example, month-to-month reserve funds, potential speculation returns, and any extra pay sources you can take advantage of.

Stage 6: Foster a financial plan: Make a far-reaching spending plan that lines up with your goals. Dispense assets for important costs, reserve funds, and speculations. Be aware of superfluous spending and track down chances to scale back and divert assets towards your goals.

Stage 7: Screen and change your arrangement: Routinely audit and assess your monetary arrangement. Keep tabs on your development, make vital changes, and adjust to evolving conditions. Be adaptable and open to adjusting your methodology on a case-by-case basis.

Keep in mind, fabricating major areas of strength for an establishment requires discipline, persistence, and consistency. By characterizing clear goals and making a practical monetary arrangement, you set before yourself the way towards monetary success and a solid future.

3

Budgeting Nuts and Bolts: Following Pay and Costs

Budgeting is an essential expertise that each young grown-up ought to dominate to deal with their funds successfully. By following your pay and costs, you can acquire a reasonable comprehension of where your cash is proceeding to settle on informed conclusions about saving and spending. Here are some budgeting essentials to assist you with the beginning:

1. Compute Your Pay: The most important phase in budgeting is to decide your pay. This incorporates all wellsprings of cash you get consistently, like your compensation, independent work, and some other side gigs. It's essential to have a reasonable image of the amount of cash you possess to work with every month.

2. Classify Your Costs: Next, order your costs into various classifications like lodging, transportation, food, diversion, and reserve funds. This will assist you with understanding where your cash is being dispensed and recognize regions where you might possibly scale back.

3. Track Your Costs: Begin following your costs by recording all that you spend. This should be possible physically utilizing a notepad or calculation sheet, or you can utilize different budgeting applications or online instruments that can consequently sort your costs for you. The key is to be steady and tireless in monitoring even the littlest costs.

4. Separate Among Needs and Needs: Separating between needs and needs is vital for successful budgeting. Needs are fundamental costs like lease, utilities, food, and transportation, while needs are trivial things like eating out or purchasing new garments. Investigate your costs and assess in the event that there are any regions where you can diminish spending on needs to dispense more towards reserve funds or other monetary goals.

5. Put forth Practical Monetary Goals: Budgeting turns out to be more significant when you have explicit monetary goals at the top of the priority list. Whether it's putting something aside for a secret stash, taking care of educational loans, or putting something aside for an upfront instalment on a house, having goals assists you with remaining spurred and centred. Put forth sensible goals that you can accomplish within a particular timeframe and integrate them into your financial plan.

6. Survey and Change: Consistently audit your spending plan to check whether you are adhering to your arranged costs and gaining ground towards your goals. Assuming you notice any regions where you are reliably overspending, distinguish procedures to decrease costs in that class. Moreover, as your pay or costs change, make vital acclimations to your financial plan to mirror these changes.

7. Fabricate a Secret stash: One fundamental piece of budgeting is building a just-in-case account. Plan to save.

Viable Ways to set aside Cash for Young Adults

As a young grown-up, setting aside cash is a significant expertise to develop right off the bat. Here are a few commonsense tips that can assist you with exploring your funds and fabricating areas of strength for your future:

1. Figure out Your Pay and costs: Find an opportunity to grasp your pay and costs. Make a month-to-month financial plan that frames your pay sources (like compensation or remittances) and your decent costs (like lease, utilities, and understudy loan instalments). Knowing where your cash is going will assist you with arriving at informed conclusions about saving and spending.

2. Begin a Backup stash: Laying out a backup stash ought to be important. Plan to save somewhere around three to a half years of everyday costs. Having this pad will give you monetary security and safeguard you if there should be an occurrence of unforeseen occasions like health-related crises or employment cutbacks.

3. Limit Eating Out: Eating out can rapidly deplete your spending plan. Attempt to restrict eating out to exceptional events and, on second thought, centre around preparing feasts at home. In addition to the fact that it is better, it's more financially savvy. Consider dinner arranging, purchasing food in mass, and getting ready feasts ahead of time to set aside both time and cash.

4. Keep away from Motivation Purchasing: Prior to making a buy, particularly for unimportant things, stop and inquire whether it's something you really need or on the other hand, if it's simply an off-the-cuff drive. Consider sitting tight for 24 hours prior to making the buy to guarantee it lines up with your monetary goals.

5. Save money on Transportation Expenses: If conceivable, think about utilizing public transportation, carpooling, or trekking to save money on transportation costs. Claiming a vehicle can be costly, with costs like gas, protection, and upkeep. Also, consider utilizing applications or sites to analyze costs and find the best arrangements for flights, transport tickets, or rental vehicles while arranging trips.

6. Track down Reasonable Lodging: Lodging can be one of the main costs for young adults. Think about offering a rental space to flatmates to divide the expenses. Search for reasonable choices that fit affordable enough for you and abstain from overspending on lodging costs.

7. Use Understudy Limits: Exploit understudy limits presented by different retailers, eateries, and diversion settings. Continuously convey your understudy ID and ask about limits any place you go. This can assist you with getting a good deal on ordinary buys and exercises.

8. Save money on Utilities: Be aware of your utility utilization by switching out lights, turning off gadgets when not being used, and utilizing energy-effective apparatuses

4

Clearing Debts and Overseeing Credit

In order to effectively manage debt, it is important to first understand the different types of debt that young adults may face. The three main types of debt are secured, unsecured, and revolving debt.

Secured debt is debt that is secured by an asset, such as a home or car. These types of loans typically have lower interest rates than unsecured debt, but the borrower risks losing the asset if they are unable to make payments.

Debt without collateral is an obligation that isn't gotten by a resource. These types of loans typically have higher interest rates than secured debt, but less risk for the borrower since there is no collateral at stake.

Revolving debt is debt that can be paid off and then borrowed again. Examples include credit cards and personal lines of credit. These types of debts can be more difficult to manage since they do not have a set repayment term and the interest rates can be high.

Strategies for Debt Repayment

Once young adults understand the types of debt they are facing, there are several strategies they can use to effectively repay their debt. One common strategy is the debt snowball method, which involves paying off the smallest debts first and then moving on to larger debts. This can help provide a sense of accomplishment and motivation.

Another strategy is the debt avalanche method, which involves paying off debts with the highest interest rates first. This can save money on interest in the long run, but may take longer to see progress.

Consolidating debt through a personal loan or balance transfer credit card can also help young adults manage their debt. However, it is important to carefully evaluate the terms and fees associated with these options.

Establishing and Maintaining Good Credit

Finally, establishing and maintaining good credit is essential for young adults looking to invest in their future. This involves making payments on time, staying within credit limits, and monitoring credit reports for errors or fraudulent activity.

One way to establish credit is through a secured credit card, which requires a deposit as collateral. This can help young adults build credit without the risk of overspending.

In addition, it is important to regularly check credit scores and ensure that they are accurate. This can help young adults identify areas for improvement and take steps to improve their credit scores over time.

Overall, understanding different types of debt, strategies for debt repayment, and establishing and maintaining good credit are important investment opportunities for young adults looking to build a strong financial   future.

5

Exploring Investment Basics

Young adults looking to invest in their future can start by exploring the investment basics, including investment fundamentals, stocks, bonds, and mutual funds, and understanding risk and return.

Investment Fundamentals

Investment fundamentals include understanding the basic concepts of investing, such as diversification, asset allocation, and investing for the long term. Diversification involves investing in a variety of assets to spread risk and increase the potential for returns. Asset allocation involves dividing investments across asset classes, such as stocks, bonds, and real estate, to further diversify investments. Investing for the long term involves taking a buy-and-hold approach, rather than trying to time the market.

Introduction to Stocks, Bonds, and Mutual Funds

Stocks, bonds, and mutual funds are common investment options for young adults. Stocks represent ownership in a company and can offer the potential for growth, but also come with higher risk. Bonds are a type of debt investment that pays interest over time and can provide a steady income stream but with a lower potential for growth. Mutual funds are a portfolio of investments across different stocks and bonds and provide instant diversification to investors.

Risk and Return: Finding Your Investment Comfort Zone

Investing involves taking on risk and understanding the relationship between risk and return is important for young adults. Higher-risk investments, such as stocks, can provide higher potential returns but are also more volatile and subject to market fluctuations. Lower-risk investments, such as bonds, provide lower potential returns but are less volatile. Understanding personal investment goals and risk tolerance can help young adults find their investment comfort zone.

Overall, exploring investment basics, including investment fundamentals, types of investments, and understanding risk and return, can provide young adults with a foundation for making informed investment decisions.

6

Investment Record Types

This makes sense of the vital contrasts between these records, including their commitment limits, qualification prerequisites, and expense suggestions. We talk about how Customary IRAs offer duty-conceded development, where commitments are charge deductible, and withdrawals are burdened in retirement. Then again, Roth IRAs give tax-exempt development, with commitments made after-charge, and qualified withdrawals are tax-exempt. We feature the benefits and contemplations of each kind and give direction on picking the right IRA in light of individual conditions and monetary goals.

401(k) and Manager Supported Plans

In this segment, This investigate business supported retirement plans, with a specific spotlight on the famous 401(k) account. We make sense of how 401(k) plans work, the significance of manager matching commitments, and the likely advantages of adding to these plans. We examine commitment limits, vesting plans, and the different venture choices accessible inside a 401(k) plan. Also, we address other manager supported plans, for example, 403(b) plans for specific philanthropic associations and 457 designs for government representatives. We give experiences into the upsides of using these designs for retirement investment funds and techniques to boost their advantages.

Available Money market funds

This analysis is available money market funds, which offer adaptability and openness for speculations. This makes sense of the essentials of opening and dealing with a money market fund, including picking a business firm, understanding exchange expenses, and executing exchanges. We examine the different speculation choices accessible inside available money market funds, for example, stocks, securities, trade exchanged reserves (ETFs), and shared reserves. We feature the assessment suggestions related to available money market funds, including capital additions expenses and profit charges. Moreover, we give direction on using these records actually, including procedures for charge-effective investing and portfolio expansion.

By giving itemized data on these speculation account types, perusers will acquire a complete comprehension of the choices accessible to them and be prepared to go with informed choices in light of their monetary goals, risk   resilience,   and   expense   contemplations.

7

Diversification and Resource Portion

The Significance of Diversifying Investments

This investigates why tying up your resources in one place can be dangerous and the way in which diversification can assist with alleviating that gamble. We talk about the advantages of diversification, like decreasing instability and possibly expanding by and large returns.

Procedures for Distributing Resources

The resource portion is the most common way of choosing how to circulate investments across various resource classes, like stocks, bonds, land, and wares. This segment centers around different systems for designating resources in light of individual goals, risk resilience, and investment skyline.

1 Current Portfolio Hypothesis and the Effective Outskirts

This present the idea of the Current Portfolio Hypothesis (MPT) and make sense of how it can direct resource designation choices. We examine the Productive Wilderness, a graphical portrayal that shows the ideal portfolios that give the most significant yields to a given degree of hazard. We give experience in developing an enhanced portfolio in light of this system.

2 Gamble-Based Resource Portion

Here, this investigate risk-based resource portion systems, like the moderate, adjusted, and forceful methodologies. We make sense of how risk resilience assumes a critical part in deciding the resource portion blend. We talk about the upsides and downsides of every methodology and give directions on picking the suitable one in light of individual conditions.

3 Age-Based Resource Designation

This part centres on resource assignment procedures that think about a singular's age and time skyline. We talk about how resource allotment ought to develop as financial backers progress through various life stages, underlining the significance of changing gamble openness and diversification as retirement draws near.

4 Strategic Resource Portion

Strategic resource allotment includes effectively changing portfolio assignments in light of momentary economic situations or investment potential open doors. We investigate different strategic designation procedures, for example, market timing and area pivot, and examine the possible advantages and dangers related to these methodologies.

5 Long haul Resource Allotment and Rebalancing

This stress the meaning of keeping a restrained way to deal with resource designation over the long haul. We make sense of the idea of rebalancing, which includes intermittently realigning portfolio allotments to their unique targets. We examine the advantages of rebalancing as far as hazard control and portfolio advancement.

By completely understanding the significance of diversification and different resource distribution methodologies, young financial backers can foster an even investment portfolio that lines up with their monetary goals, risk resistance, and investment skyline.

8

Securities Exchange Investing

This part digs into the thrilling universe of securities exchange investing, which offers young adults an abundance of chances to develop their abundance over the long run. We investigate the essential ideas and systems that can assist young financial backers with pursuing educated choices and expanding their possibilities regarding success.

Principal Investigation and Stock Choice

Understanding principal examination is essential for young financial backers who mean to make brilliant stock determinations. We make sense of the vital components of the central examination, including assessing an organization's monetary well-being, dissecting its serious situation on the lookout, and evaluating its development potential. We additionally dig into the most common way of leading exhaustive exploration and an expected level of effort on likely investments.

Besides, this part gives pragmatic direction on the most proficient method to assess budget summaries, break down key monetary proportions, and decipher income reports. By dominating these abilities, young financial backers can distinguish underestimated stocks and pursue informed choices in view of the drawn-out capability of the organizations they put resources into.

Investigating Different Investment Systems

This subsection acquaints young adults with different investment systems that can be applied in the financial exchange. We investigate both conventional methodologies, featuring their interesting qualities, risk profiles, and likely returns. A portion of the investment systems shrouded in this segment include:

a) **Worth Investing:** We make sense of the standards behind esteem investing, promoted by eminent financial backer Warren Buffett. Young financial backers will figure out how to recognize underestimated stocks and exploit market shortcomings to produce long-haul returns.

b) **Development Investing:** We investigate the idea of development investing, zeroing in on organizations with high development potential. Young financial backers will comprehend how to recognize promising businesses and organizations ready for significant extension, permitting them to gain through future development.

c) **Profit Investing:** We examine the advantages of profit investing, which includes investing in organizations that reliably appropriate profits to their investors. Young adults will find out about the significance of profit yield, payout proportions, and profit development while choosing stocks for money age and long haul abundance aggregation.

d) **File Asset Investing:** We feature the upsides of record store investing, especially for young adults who favour a more latent methodology. We make sense of how file supports offer expansive market openness, diversification, and low expenses, making them an appealing choice for those searching for a hands-off investment technique.

e) **Area Revolution:** We present the idea of area turn, which includes decisively moving investments between various areas in view of market patterns and financial cycles. Young financial backers will figure out how to distinguish areas ready for development and position their portfolios appropriately.

By investigating these different investment systems, young adults can foster a balanced comprehension of the securities exchange and pick moves that line up with their gamble resilience, monetary goals, and individual inclinations.

9

Real Estate Investing

Real estate investing presents a wealth of opportunities for young adults looking to invest in their future. It's a tangible asset that can appreciate in value over time, provide rental income, and diversify one's investment portfolio. Below are some investment options and steps to get started in real estate investing.

Understanding Real Estate Investment Options

Real estate investment options can vary based on the amount of capital available to invest and the level of involvement desired by the investor. Here are some popular options:

1 Rental Properties: Purchasing a rental property can provide a steady income stream through monthly rents and long-term appreciation. Young adults can start by purchasing a small multi-family property or a single-family home to rent out.

2 Real Estate Investment Trusts (REITs): REITs are securities that own and manage real estate properties, offering investors a way to invest in real estate without owning physical properties. REITs can provide diversification and steady income, while eliminating the need for active property management.

3 Land Crowdfunding: Land crowdfunding stages permit financial backers to pool their cash to put resources into land projects. These stages normally have lower investment essentials and can give admittance to bigger arrangements that may not be accessible to individual financial backers.

Moves toward Getting everything rolling in Land Investing

Getting started in real estate investing can be daunting, but here are some steps to consider:

1 Build a Strong Financial Foundation: Before investing, young adults should establish a strong financial foundation, including paying off high-interest debt, creating an emergency fund, and saving for retirement.

2 Educate Yourself: It's important to educate yourself on the real estate market, investment strategies, and potential risks. Consider reading books, attending seminars and workshops, and networking with other investors.

3 Set Investment Goals: Determine investment goals and develop a strategy that aligns with those goals. Will you invest for cash flow, appreciation, or a combination of both?

4 Financing: Determine how you will finance your investment property. Young adults may have access to low down-payment mortgage options like FHA loans. It's important to consider the costs associated with owning a property, such as property taxes, maintenance costs, and insurance.

5 Find the Right Property: Research markets and neighbourhoods to determine where to buy, and search for a property that aligns with your investment goals. Analyze the property's cash flow potential, and consider hiring a professional inspector to identify any potential issues.

In conclusion, investing in real estate can be an excellent investment opportunity for young adults looking to build wealth over time. Understanding real estate investment options and following the steps to get started can help young adults successfully navigate the real estate investing landscape.

10

Peer-to-Peer Lending and Crowdfunding

E‌xploring the World of Peer-to-Peer Lending

Peer-to-peer lending, also known as P2P lending, is a form of alternative lending that connects borrowers directly with lenders through an online platform. In P2P lending, borrowers apply for loans through an online platform, and investors can then fund these loans in exchange for interest on their investments. P2P lending has become a popular way for individuals to lend and borrow money outside of traditional financial institutions.

One benefit of P2P lending is that it offers borrowers a way to access funding quickly and easily, while also allowing investors to earn attractive returns on their investments. P2P lending platforms typically charge lower fees than traditional financial institutions, making it an attractive option for both borrowers and investors.

However, P2P lending also comes with risks. Investments are not FDIC-insured, and borrowers may default on loans, leading to losses for investors. It's important for investors to research P2P lending platforms and assess the creditworthiness of borrowers before investing.

Investing in Crowdfunded Projects and Startups

Crowdfunding is a method of raising money from a large number of people, typically through an online platform. Crowdfunding offers entrepreneurs a way to raise capital for their projects or startups, often from a diverse set of investors who are passionate about their idea.

Investors can participate in crowdfunding by investing in equity-based crowdfunding campaigns, in which they receive equity in the company in exchange for their investment, or by investing in debt-based crowdfunding campaigns, in which they receive interest on their investment. Crowdfunding campaigns typically have a set funding goal and time frame, and investors can contribute funds until the goal is reached.

Crowdfunding can offer investors an opportunity to invest in innovative and potentially high-growth startups, but it also comes with risks. The success of a crowdfunding campaign and the startup it supports are not guaranteed. Investors should research potential crowdfunding campaigns and assess the management team, market opportunity, and competitive landscape before investing.

In conclusion, P2P lending and crowdfunding offer alternative investment opportunities outside of traditional financial institutions. These methods of investing can provide attractive returns, but they also come with risks. It's important for investors to conduct research and assess potential investments carefully before making any investment decisions.

11

Impact Investing and Socially Responsible Investing

Impact investing and socially responsible investing (SRI) have gained popularity in recent years as investors aim to align their investments with their personal values and contribute to positive social and environmental impacts. Here are two key aspects of impact investing and SRI: aligning investments with personal values, and evaluating impacts and measurable returns.

1. Aligning Investments with Personal Values:

One of the core principles of impact investing and SRI is aligning investments with personal values. Many investors want their investments to reflect their values and support social and environmental causes they care about. For example, some investors may want to invest in companies that prioritize sustainability and renewable energy, while others may prioritize investing in businesses that promote diversity and inclusion.

There are different approaches to aligning investments with personal values. One is to invest in mutual funds and exchange-traded funds (ETFs) that prioritize companies with strong sustainability and social responsibility ratings. These funds conduct research on companies' environmental, social, and governance (ESG) practices to ensure they are meeting certain ethical and sustainable standards.

Another approach is to invest in individual companies that align with personal values. This approach may require more research and due diligence, as investors will need to examine companies' practices and values to ensure they are in alignment.

2. Evaluating Impacts and Measurable Returns:

Another key aspect of impact investing and SRI is evaluating impacts and measurable returns. While the social and environmental impacts of investments can be difficult to measure, it's important to evaluate investments based on more than just financial returns.

One way to evaluate the impact of investments is to look at the outcomes and outputs of the investments. Outcomes refer to the long-term impact or changes that result from the investment, while outputs refer to the immediate results or benefits of the investment. For example, an outcome of investing in solar energy may be a reduction in carbon emissions, while an output may be the immediate increase in renewable energy production.

Impact investors and those focused on SRI also use key performance indicators (KPIs) to measure the social and environmental impacts of their investments. KPIs are metrics that help investors understand and measure the progress and success of their investments. Examples of KPIs may include reductions in greenhouse gas emissions, increased access to healthcare, or improvements in worker safety and labor practices.

In conclusion, impact investing and SRI offer investors a way to align their investments with their personal values and contribute to positive social and environmental impacts. Evaluating impacts and measurable returns, as well as aligning investments with personal values, are important considerations for investors interested in impact investing and SRI.

12

Exploring Alternative Investment

Investing in Cryptocurrency and Blockchain Technology

Digital currency is a computerized resource intended to function as a vehicle of trade that utilizes cryptography to get its exchanges and to control the production of extra units. Blockchain technology is the underlying technology behind most cryptocurrencies and is a decentralized, distributed ledger that records transactions on multiple computers in a tamper-proof, secure way.

Cryptocurrency has been a popular alternative investment option in recent years, with investors seeking potentially high returns in a relatively short amount of time. However, the cryptocurrency market is highly volatile and prices can fluctuate rapidly, making it a risky investment for many investors.

Investors interested in cryptocurrency should conduct thorough research to understand the market and the various cryptocurrencies available. They should also consider the risks involved and use caution when investing. Some investors choose to purchase and hold cryptocurrency for the long term, while others engage in trading and speculation.

Art Collectibles and Other Tangible Assets

Art, collectables, and other tangible assets are alternative investments that can provide diversification to a portfolio. These assets can include artwork, vintage wine, jewellery, coins, and even rare books. Tangible assets can appreciate in value over time and provide a store of value that is not affected by market volatility.

However, investing in tangible assets can also be risky. The value of these assets is subject to fluctuations in the market and can be affected by changes in taste and demand. Investors interested in tangible assets should do their research and seek professional advice before investing.

There are also costs associated with owning and storing tangible assets, such as insurance and security. Investors may also face challenges when selling these assets, as they may need to find a buyer who is willing to pay a fair price.

In conclusion, investing in cryptocurrency and blockchain technology, as well as art collectables and other tangible assets, can be attractive alternative investment options. However, investors should carefully consider the risks and potential rewards before investing in these areas. They should also conduct thorough research and seek professional advice before making any investment decisions.

13

Overseeing Hazard and Feelings

Investing implies innate dangers, and understanding how to deal with these dangers is essential for young adults looking for long-haul monetary development. This part of the book centres around two key perspectives: understanding risk and volatility, and addressing the psychological factors that can influence investment decisions.

Understanding Risk and Volatility

Defining Risk and Volatility

a. Risk: Risk refers to the potential for loss or negative outcome when making an investment. It can include factors such as market fluctuations, economic conditions, industry-specific risks, and company-specific risks.

b. Volatility: Volatility measures the rate at which the price of an investment rises or falls. It is a measure of the potential price swings or fluctuations in the market. Higher volatility often indicates higher risk, but it can also present opportunities for higher returns.

2. The Relationship between Risk and Return

a. Risk-Reward Trade-off: Generally, investments with higher levels of risk have the potential for higher returns. However, it's important to assess your risk tolerance and financial goals before choosing an investment strategy. Remember, what works for one person may not work for another.

b. Diversification: One way to manage risk is through diversification. By spreading your investments across different asset classes (such as stocks, bonds, and real estate) and within those classes (for example, investing in different industries or geographic regions), you can potentially reduce the impact of any single investment's performance on your overall portfolio.

3. Evaluating Risk and Volatility

a. Time Horizon: Consider your investment time horizon before making decisions. Young adults generally have a longer time horizon, giving them the advantage of riding out market fluctuations and allowing investments to potentially grow over time.

b. Research and Analysis: Do thorough research on the investment opportunities you're considering. Understand the underlying fundamentals of the investments, such as company financials, industry trends, and market dynamics. This will help you make informed decisions, reducing the risk of potential losses.

c. Seek Professional Advice: Consider seeking guidance from financial advisors or investment professionals who can help you understand the risks associated with different investments. They can provide personalized advice based on your risk profile and financial goals.

14

Tax Considerations for Investors

Tax-proficient Investing Systems

Grasping the Significance of Tax Productivity: Realize the reason why tax effectiveness is essential for augmenting investment returns.

1 Tax-Advantaged Records: Investigate various sorts of tax-advantaged investment accounts, like IRAs and 401(k)s, and comprehend how they can assist with decreasing your tax trouble.

2 Resource Area: Find the idea of resource area and how decisively setting investments in various kinds of records can advance tax productivity.

3 Tax-Proficient Asset Determination: Figure out how to recognize tax-effective common assets and trade exchanged reserves (ETFs) to limit taxable dissemination.

4 Tax-Misfortune Gathering: Investigate the idea of tax-misfortune reaping and how it tends to be utilized to counterbalance capital gains and decrease taxes.

5 Isolated and Capital Addition Techniques: Comprehend how to oversee profits and capital increases to limit the tax influence.

6 Timing Methodologies: Find techniques, for example, tax-misfortune selling and tax-gain reaping to make the most of timing open doors inside the tax code.

7 Contemplations for Global Financial Backers: Investigate tax contemplations intended for worldwide financial backers and techniques for limiting tax liabilities.

Augmenting Tax Advantages and Limiting Liabilities

1 Tax Allowances and Credits: Find out about tax derivations and credits accessible to financial backers, for example, deducting investment-related expenses and using tax credits for explicit investment exercises.

2 Retirement Commitments: Comprehend the tax advantages of adding to retirement accounts and augmenting commitments to decrease taxable pay.

3 Bequest Arranging and Tax Enhancement: Find how domain arranging can assist with limiting taxes and guarantee a smooth exchange of abundance to beneficiaries.

4 Altruistic Commitments: Find out about tax benefits connected with magnanimous giving and how to advance your commitments.

5 Figuring out Tax Regulations and Changes: Remain informed about the most recent tax regulations and guidelines that might influence your investments and tax liabilities.

6 Looking for Proficient Tax Counsel: Comprehend when it could be gainful to talk with a tax proficient to guarantee you are boosting tax benefits and limiting liabilities in your investment methodology.

By diving into tax-productive investing systems and investigating ways of boosting tax benefits while limiting liabilities, young financial backers can advance their investment returns and accomplish long haul monetary goals all the more successfully. Understanding and carrying out these tax contemplations will assist perusers with exploring the intricacies of the tax framework and settle on informed choices to help their investment success.

15

Long-Term Investing and Retirement Planning

Strategies for Long-Term Wealth Accumulation

Long-term wealth accumulation is the process of building wealth over a period through consistent savings and smart investment decisions. Here are some strategies for long-term wealth accumulation:

1 Start early: The earlier you start investing, the better off you will be in the long term. Investing in your 20s and 30s can give you a significant advantage due to the power of compounding.

2 Diversify your portfolio: Invest in a mix of stocks, bonds, and other investment products to diversify your portfolio and reduce risk.

3 Use tax-advantaged accounts: Take advantage of tax-advantaged accounts like 401(k)s and IRAs to save for retirement and reduce your taxable income.

4 Invest for the long-term: Avoid short-term thinking when it comes to investing and focus on long-term goals.

5 Stay disciplined: Stick to your investment strategy, even during market downturns, and avoid emotional decision-making.

Retirement Planning Essentials

Planning for retirement is an essential part of long-term investing. Here are some retirement planning essentials:

1 Determine your retirement goals: Calculate how much you will need to save for retirement based on your lifestyle and expenses.

2 Start saving early: Begin saving for retirement as early as possible to take advantage of the power of compounding.

3 Use tax-advantaged accounts: Invest in tax-advantaged accounts like 401(k)s and IRAs to maximize your retirement savings.

4 Consider your risk tolerance: Determine your risk tolerance when investing for retirement and adjust your investments accordingly.

5 Review and adjust your plan: Regularly review and adjust your retirement plan to ensure you stay on track to meet your retirement goals.

6 Plan for healthcare expenses: Plan for healthcare expenses in retirement by considering Medicare and other healthcare options.

Investment Opportunities for Young Adults

Young adults have a long-term investment horizon and can take advantage of investment opportunities that offer growth potential. Here are some investment opportunities for young adults:

1 Stock: Investing in individual stocks or index funds can offer growth potential over the long term.

2 Real estate: Investing in real estate can offer growth potential and provide diversification to a portfolio.

3 Start a business: Starting a business can offer significant growth potential and provide an opportunity for young adults to pursue their passions.

4 Alternative investments: Investing in alternative investments like cryptocurrency, art, and collectables can offer growth potential, but also come with higher risk.

5 Education: Investing in education can provide young adults with the skills and knowledge to pursue career opportunities and increase earning potential over time.

16

Conclusion

In "Seizing Success: Investment Opportunities for Young Adults," we have investigated the universe of investing and given an extensive manual for assist you with pursuing informed monetary choices. From understanding the force of investing to investigating different investment opportunities, we have outfitted you with the information and techniques important to leave on your investment process.

We started by stressing the significance of building areas of strength for an establishment, laying out goals, budgeting, and overseeing obligations. By laying out great monetary propensities from the beginning, you have laid the foundation for a successful investment venture.

We then dug into investment rudiments, including different resource classes and investment account types. Diversification and resource designation were featured as key standards to oversee risk and enhance returns. Furnished with this information, you can certainly explore the investment scene and pursue informed choices that line up with your monetary goals.

All through the book, we exhibited a scope of investment opportunities reasonable for young adults. From financial exchange investing to land, shared loaning, and effect investing, we investigated both customary and elective roads for abundance creation. We meant to move you to think past conventional investment choices and consider opportunities that line up with your interests and values.

Besides, we committed a segment to tending to the difficulties that might emerge during your investment process. Overseeing risk, defeating close to home predispositions, and understanding tax contemplations were examined to assist you with exploring likely entanglements. We likewise focused on the meaning of long haul investing and retirement arranging, directing you on techniques to collect abundance and secure your monetary future.

As you close this book, recollect that investing is a deep rooted educational experience. Markets advance, new opportunities arise, and individual conditions change. It is vital to remain informed, adjust your techniques depending on the situation, and look for proficient guidance when important.

With the information and apparatuses gave in this book, you are exceptional to quickly take advantage of the investment chances that lie ahead. By settling on sound monetary choices and remaining focused on your drawn out goals, you can make ready for monetary freedom and a prosperous future.

This is the ideal opportunity to make a move, embrace the universe of investing, and set out on your excursion toward monetary success. Take advantage of the chances, beat difficulties, and let your investments work for you. May this book act as an important asset and guide on your way to monetary strengthening and long haul abundance gathering.

www.ingramcontent.com/pod-product-compliance
Lightning Source LLC
Chambersburg PA
CBHW070857220526
45466CB00005B/2027